QUIT SMART™

STOP SMOKING

With the QuitSmart System,
It's easier than you think!

Dr. Robert H. Shipley

with a section
by Dr. Jed Rose

QuitSmart Stop Smoking Resources, Inc., P.O. Box 99016, Duke Station, Durham, NC 27708-9016, (919) 644-0736 (For ordering information, please turn to the last page). Visit our home page at www.QuitSmart.com

ISBN numbers:
1-880781-99-9	1999 QuitSmart Stop Smoking Guide
1-880781-48-4	1999 QuitSmart Stop Smoking Kit (includes QuitSmart Guide, Hypnosis Tape, and Cigarette Substitute.)

Printed in the United States of America

Cover Design by Jamie Sanders

Typesetting by Melody Merritt/9th Street Type & Design, Inc.

What the professionals are saying about QuitSmart:

"Dr. Robert Shipley, director of the prestigious Duke University Quit Smoking Clinic, has come up with a tool to help people through the struggle. . . . The appealing prose, cartoons and charts make for engaging reading."

Mark J. Tager, M.D.
American Journal of Health Promotion

"Advice on how to quit smoking is easy to come by. This book, however, is considerably more than mere advice. It represents the results of many years of research on methods for successful quitting."

Patrick A. Boudewyns, Ph.D.
Professor, Department of Psychiatry
    and Health Behavior
Medical College of Georgia

"A remarkably clear, practical guide to assist those who want to stop smoking!"

John R. Feussner, M.D.
Director, Center for Health Services
    Research in Primary Care
Department of Veterans Affairs

"The QuitSmart book and tape are terrific. It is the finest, most useful tool I've ever seen to help smokers quit. I'm recommending it to all my patients who are smokers."

Belinda R. Novik, Ph.D.
Practicing Clinical Psychologist
Past President, North Carolina Society
    of Clinical Hypnosis

"The QuitSmart Stop Smoking Kit is easy to use, interactive, and informative . . . I enthusiastically recommend the kit.

Crystal L. Dunlevy, Ed.D., RRT
Respiratory Care Journal

To Alice, Kim, Jennifer, Kendall,
and
to the thousands of people who
allowed me to share their journey
to freedom from cigarettes.

Preface

Each day, cigarette smoking kills 9000 people worldwide. In the United States, 1300 people die each day from illness caused by smoking. That is more deaths than caused by AIDS, cocaine, heroin, alcohol, fire, automobile accidents, murders, and suicides COMBINED.

Smokers die early from heart attacks, strokes, lung cancer, emphysema, and from many other diseases. For those who die early, smoking robs them of 12 to 21 years of life. My father died of a heart attack at age 64. If he had not smoked, he might have lived to age 76 or more.

Cigarettes also rob smokers of their health, causing shortness of breath, colds, coughs, facial wrinkles, stomach ulcers, and early onset of menopause.

If you are like most smokers, you know the dangers of smoking and want to be free of cigarettes, but until recently, effective help did not exist. Now things have changed. The QuitSmart System will help you break the three chains that bind you to cigarettes: physical addiction, habit, and emotional dependence.

As Director of the QuitSmart™ Stop Smoking Clinic at Duke University Medical Center, and President of QuitSmart Stop Smoking Resources, I have seen how well the QuitSmart System works. This popular guidebook (over 100,000 copies in print) shows you how to use this powerful system to stop smoking for good.

For many people, one of the keys to success is temporary use of medication. In this guidebook, you will learn about Zyban™ pills and nicotine-replacement products (patch, gum, spray, inhaler). The information on the nicotine patch is provided by Dr. Jed Rose, a world-famous smoking-cessation researcher. Dr. Rose, along with Dr. Murray Jarvik and Dr. Daniel Rose, holds patents on the nicotine skin patch.

I am a former smoker who went through a lot of struggle before finally breaking free of cigarettes. I know that deciding to quit smoking is difficult. While part of you knows you will be better off without cigarettes, another part of you enjoys smoking and does not want to give up that pleasure. One of your first tasks in working with this guidebook will be to resolve these mixed feelings.

This guidebook presents the most up-to-date, scientific, *smart* ways to quit smoking. By reading this guide and using the suggested coping methods, you have a good chance to break free from cigarettes for good. You can do it!

Robert H. Shipley, Ph.D.

Contents

Introduction

Congratulations on your decision to break free from cigarettes! Success in this, as in most areas of life, depends on "keeping your head" and using the best methods. The QuitSmart guidebook provides the information you need. As you read and reread it, you will be able to succeed with greater ease than you thought possible.

Quitting is not so much a matter of *willpower* as it is of *skill*—doing the right things and thinking the right thoughts to make sure you succeed. In the sections that follow you will learn to:

- Develop your personal reasons for breaking free of cigarettes.

- Ease off nicotine by switching to low-nicotine cigarettes prior to quitting.

- Temporarily use one of the nicotine or non-nicotine medications to reduce withdrawal symptoms.

- Use your thoughts to make quitting easier.

- Relax during the withdrawal phase with deep breaths, physical activity, and hypnosis.

- Use a cigarette substitute to break the habit of having something in your hand and mouth.

- Ask for the support of family and friends.

- Control your weight.

- Add pleasures to your day to offset the lost pleasures of smoking.

- Avoid smoking temptations, and deal with smoking "come-ons."

- Stay free of cigarettes for life.

The chapters in this guidebook cover the three phases of quitting: *Preparing to Quit, Quitting,* and *Remaining a Nonsmoker.* During each phase of quitting, study the chapter for that phase and for the next phase. In this way, you will always be prepared with the best coping methods. When preparing to quit, for example, you should study Chapter 1, *Preparing to Quit,* and Chapter 2, *Quitting.*

Refer often to this guide. It was kept small so that you can carry it with you. Read with pencil or pen ready because you will be an active participant in this learning experience. Practice the suggested coping methods, even those that seem a bit silly or unnecessary. When you use the QuitSmart System taught in this guide, you will have a good chance of success.

Be proud of your decision to break free from cigarettes. You are already on your way to feeling better and to living a longer and healthier life!

QUIT SMART™

CHAPTER 1
Preparing to Quit

Just as you plan for a trip by thinking ahead and deciding what you will take along, this chapter will help you plan ahead for successful quitting. First, you will increase your motivation for quitting by listing your reasons for breaking free from cigarettes.

You will answer two questions to see if you are addicted to the nicotine in your cigarettes. If addicted, you can ease off nicotine before you quit smoking by switching gradually to low-nicotine brands. You will also consider using medications that can reduce withdrawal symptoms, and double your chances of long-term success.

You will learn why, once you become a nonsmoker, you may need less coffee, tea, and cola drinks. However, you will not be asked to give up caffeine entirely.

You will obtain support for your quitting efforts by asking for help from family and friends, and by "smoke proofing" your home and workplace to reduce temptation.

Finally, you will learn the importance of making a firm quitting decision, and you will select your quit date—your first day of freedom from cigarettes. Prior to quitting, you will also want to read Chapter 2, *Quitting*, so you will have effective coping methods ready to use on your quit date.

List Your Reasons for Quitting

It can be difficult to decide to quit because so many people are saying that you should quit. This pressure may be coming from all sides: government, employers, doctors, friends, and family. However, no one can make you quit. In fact, pressure can backfire, causing you to dig in your heels and think, "Those anti-smokers can't make me quit."

You may have started to smoke, in part, to show that you were in control of your own life. But are you still in control, or are you forced to smoke by your addiction to cigarettes?

To make *your* quitting decision, you will want to decide your reasons for quitting. You need strong personal reasons to give up the pleasures of smoking. Other people's reasons are not important.

Look over the reasons for quitting listed on the next page, and put a check mark by those that are your reasons. Then add additional reasons that are important to you.

Refer to your list of reasons to help you remember why you made the important personal decision to break free from cigarettes. It is a good idea to make copies of your list, and put the copies where you can see them at home and at work.

I am quitting cigarettes because:

❑ I will not have to worry so much about cancer, heart disease, and stroke.

❑ I will breathe easier.

❑ My skin will look healthier.

❑ I will have fewer colds and less congestion.

❑ I will have more energy.

❑ I will not feel like a social outcast.

❑ I will stop coughing.

❑ My children will be protected from second-hand smoke.

❑ I will no longer have to worry about starting an accidental fire.

❑ I will wake up feeling more rested.

❑ I will smell better to others.

❑ My sour stomach will improve.

❑ My house and car will be cleaner.

❑ My teeth will be whiter.

❑ My sports performance will improve.

❑ I will not have to clean dirty ashtrays.

❑ I will save lots of money.

❑ I will feel more in control of my life.

❑ _____

❑ _____

❑ _____

Are You Addicted to Nicotine?

Many smokers are addicted to the nicotine in cigarettes. If they do not smoke for a time, the nicotine level in their blood drops, and they have a strong urge for a cigarette. Answer the questions below to see if you are addicted to nicotine.*

1. How soon after you wake up do you smoke your first cigarette?

   □ Within 5 minutes   (3 points)
   □ 6-30 minutes   (2 points)
   □ 31-60 minutes   (1 point)
   □ After 60 minutes   (0 points)

2. How many cigarettes per day do you smoke?

   □ 10 or less   (0 points)
   □ 11-20   (1 point)
   □ 21-30   (2 points)
   □ 31 or more   (3 points)

The sooner that you have your first cigarette in the morning, and the more cigarettes you smoke each day, the more likely that you are addicted to nicotine.

Add up the points next to your answers. If your total score is two or less, you are not addicted to nicotine. You can quit "cold turkey."

If your score is three or more, you are addicted to nicotine. You can ease off nicotine by switching to brands of cigarettes with less nicotine before you quit. Sometimes we call this "warm chicken" quitting. It is easier than quitting cold turkey.

If addicted, in addition to switching to lower nicotine cigarettes, we suggest that you use one of the nicotine-replacement products (patch, gum, inhaler, or nasal spray) or the medication Zyban™. These medications are discussed after the next section so that you will have time before your quit date to talk to your doctor and go to the drug store.

NOTE: *Do not attempt to quit cigarettes by switching to pipes, cigars, chewing tobacco, or snuff.* Use of each of these tobacco products can be harmful to your health. Use of chewing tobacco or snuff can cause gum disease and mouth cancer.

Pipe or cigar smoking causes heart disease and lung cancer. Even those pipe or cigar smokers who believe they do not inhale the smoke are at risk. Research has shown that cigarette smokers who switch to pipe or cigar smoking inhale large amounts of smoke into their lungs.

*From Heatherton, et al., 1989 and 1991, *British Journal of Addiction*, volumes 84 and 86.

Brand Switching to Reduce Addiction

Prior to quitting, you will benefit from switching to brands of cigarettes that contain less nicotine. Find the nicotine content of your cigarettes by locating your exact brand in the table on the following pages. For example, if you smoke Marlboros, you are taking in 1.2 milligrams of nicotine in each cigarette (box 12 in the table). Other Marlboro brands (Lights and Ultra Lights) have different amounts of nicotine, so it is important to find your exact brand.

Within the box listing your cigarette brand are instructions to switch to a new box number. Select a brand from the new box and smoke it for one week. Then select a brand from the next indicated box, and smoke it during the second week. Continue this way, switching to lower-nicotine cigarettes each week, until you are smoking a brand in box 2; these brands have 0.2 milligrams of nicotine or less.

If you are smoking an average-nicotine brand (boxes 6–11), you will make two brand switches over two weeks. Smokers of high nicotine brands (boxes 12–17) make three switches—normally these switches are made over three weeks. However, participants in QuitSmart classes have just two weeks to complete the brand-switching procedure before the class quit date. Therefore, if you are in a class and are smoking a brand in boxes 12–17, you will be asked to switch brands every 4–5 days.

In smoking each lower-nicotine brand, be careful not to defeat your purpose of taking in less nicotine. Smoke no more than your usual number of cigarettes and do not inhale more deeply or smoke the cigarette further down! Be careful not to cover the ventilation holes placed around the filter of some cigarettes.

Example: Gerry smoked thirty Pall Mall Lights a day. She found this brand in box 9 (0.9 milligrams nicotine) and saw that she should switch to a brand in box 5. She selected Winston Ultra-Lights and smoked thirty of these a day for one week. For the second week she switched to Carlton Kings in box 2. Then she quit entirely, with few physical withdrawal symptoms.

Many people ask why not reduce nicotine addiction by cutting down the number of cigarettes they smoke. However, as you reduce the number of cigarettes smoked, each remaining cigarette becomes more pleasurable. It is very difficult to give up the last few cigarettes. With brand switching, each cigarette is not so pleasurable, and giving them up is much easier.

Do not switch right away to a brand lowest in nicotine. This would give you lots of physical withdrawal symptoms. Take it step by step.

Note: Smokeless tobacco users may switch from very high nicotine brands (Copenhagen Snuff®) to medium-high brands (Original Fine Cut Skoal Wintergreen®) to medium brands (Skoal Long Cut®) to low-nicotine brands (Hawken®, Kodiak®, Skoal Bandits®).

Cigarettes Grouped by Nicotine Content

Find your exact brand in one of the boxes. Below the black bar in the box you will see "Switch next to Box ..." Turn to that box and select a brand to smoke over the next week. Continue to switch brands each week. Quit after you complete box 2.

Brands are filtered except those listed as nonfilter (NF). Nicotine values listed for a brand apply to king, 100, and 120 size cigarettes and to menthol and nonmenthol varieties (unless otherwise specified).

Low-price generic and private-label store brands are included in the boxes under the name "Store Brands." See page 23 for more information and a list of store brands.

17   1.7 Milligrams Nicotine or More

Switch next to Box 9

Bristol (NF)	Natural American Spirit
Camel (NF)	Phillip Morris
Class A King (NF)	Commander (NF)
English Oval (NF)	Players (NF)

15   1.5 - 1.6 Milligrams Nicotine

Switch next to Box 8

Basic (NF)	Prime (NF)
Chesterfield Full Flavor	Pyramid (NF)
Class A Kings (NF)	Raleigh (NF)
Herbert Tareyton (NF)	Spring
Lucky Strike Regulars (NF)	*Store Brands (NF)
Old Gold Straight (NF)	Summit (NF)
Pall Mall (NF)	

13   1.3 - 1.4 Milligrams Nicotine

Switch next to Box 7

Camel 99's
Chesterfield Kings (NF)
Class A Full Flavor
Class A Regular (NF)
Covington Full Flavor
Kool Regular (NF)
Newport
Newport Ice

Philip Morris Regular (NF)
Private Stock (NF)
Pyramid Full Flavor
Raleigh Plains
Richland 100's
Salem
Tall 120's

12   1.2 Milligrams Nicotine

Switch next to Box 6

American
Camel
Camel Wides
Chesterfield Lights
Dakota Full Flavor
Doral (NF)
Dunhill
Kamel Red
Kool
Lark Full Flavor
Lucky Strike
Marlboro
Max 120's

Monarch (NF)
Montclair
Pall Mall Gold
Pall Mall Red
Philip Morris International
Picayune (NF)
Raleigh Extra (NF)
Saratoga 120's
Special 10's
Viceroy
Winston
Winston Select

Remember, for each brand of cigarettes, the nicotine content listed applies to all lengths of that brand (kings, 100s, 120s) and to menthol and nonmenthol varieties of that brand (unless otherwise specified). Low-price store brands and generic cigarettes are all listed as "store brands."

11   1.1 Milligrams Nicotine

Switch next to Box 5

Alpine	Kool Kings
Benson and Hedges	Misty Slims
Bristol Full Flavor	More
Bull Durham	Old Gold
Cambridge Full Flavor	Prime
Crowns	Private Stock
Chesterfield Regular (NF)	Richland Kings
Class A Deluxe Full Flavor	*Store Brands Full Flavor
Class A Lights	Summit
Eve Light 120's	Virginia Slims 100's
Hi-Lite	Virginia Slims Light 120's

10   1.0 Milligrams Nicotine

Switch next to Box 5

American Lights	Lark Lights
Basic	Malibu Lights
Bucks	Maverick Specials
Capri 120's	Montclair Lights
Class A Deluxe Lights	Newport Stripes
Covington Lights	Raleigh
Eve Slim Light 100's	Raleigh Extra
GPC	Satin
Harley-Davidson	Tareyton
Jasmine Slims	Turney Slims
L & M	

Remember, for each brand of cigarettes, the nicotine content listed applies to all lengths of that brand (kings, 100s, 120s) and to menthol and nonmenthol varieties of that brand (unless otherwise specified). Low-price store brands and generic cigarettes are all listed as "store brands."

9   0.9 Milligrams Nicotine

Switch next to Box 5

Benson and Hedges Multi
Bristol Lights
Cambridge Lights
Camel Wides Lights
Camel Lights
Camel Special Lights
Dakota Lights
Doral Full Flavor
Generic Lights
Heritage Lights
Kamel Red Lights
Kent
Lucky Strike Lights
Magna
Monarch
More White Lights
Pall Mall Lights
Players
Prime Lights
Private Stock Lights
Pyramid Lights
Raleigh Lights
Richland Lights
Silva Thins
Special 10's Lights
Sterling Full Flavor
Style Lights
Summit Lights
Marlboro Medium
Viceroy Lights

8   0.8 Milligrams Nicotine

Switch next to Box 4

Basic Lights
Benson & Hedges Lights
Capri Super Slim Lights
Crowns Lights
Chelsea
Falcon Lights
Golden Lights
Horizon Lights
Kent Golden Lights
Kent Slim Lights
Kool Milds
Marlboro Lights
Magna
Misty Slims Lights
More Lights
Newport Ice Lights
Newport Lights
Newport Slim Lights
Old Gold Lights
Parliament Lights
Players Lights
Raleigh Extra Full Flavor
Ritz
Salem Lights
Salem Slim Lights
Spring Lights
*StoreBrands—Lights
Style Slim Lights
Winston Lights
Winston Select Lights
Winston Select Slim Lights

7   0.7 Milligrams Nicotine

Switch next to Box 4

Alpine Lights
Belair
Bucks Lights
Capri 100's
Cartier Vendome
Century Lights
Class A Ultra-Lights
Doral Lights
GPC Lights

Harley-Davidson Lights
Jasmine Slim Lights
Maverick Special Lights
Merit
Raleigh Extra—Lights
Sterling Lights
Tourney Slim Lights
Vantage
Virginia Slims Lights 100's

6   0.6 Milligrams Nicotine

Switch next to Box 4

Bristol Ultra-Lights
Covington Ultra-Lights
Crowns Ultra-Lights
Generic Ultra-Lights
Kool Lights
Magna Lights
Malibu Ultra Lights

Monarch Lights
Montclair Ultra-Lights
Private Stock Ultra-Lights
Tareyton Lights
True 100's
Summit Ultra-Lights

5   0.5 Milligrams Nicotine

Switch next to Box 2

Basic Ultra-Lights
Camel Ultra-Lights
Capri Ultra-Lights
Carlton 120s
Century
Class A Deluxe Ultra-Lights
Eve Slim Ultra-Lights
Eve Ultra-Lights
GPC Ultra-Lights
Marlboro Ultra Lights

Merit Ultra-Lights
Misty Slims Ultra-Lights
Prime Ultra-Lights
Pyramid Ultra-Lights
Sterling Slim Lights
*Store Brands Ultra-Lights
Virginia Slims 100's
  Ultra-Lights
Virginia Super Slims 100's
Winston Ultra-Lights

4 — 0.4 Milligrams Nicotine

Switch next to Box 2

Barclay
Benson and Hedges Delux
  Ultra-Lights
Cambridge Ultra-Lights
Doral Ultra-Lights
Kent III
Kool Ultra
Monarch Ultra-Lights

Raleigh Extra Ultra-Lights
Salem Ultra-Lights
Sterling Ultra-Lights
Style Ultra-Lights
Triumph
True Kings
Vantage Ultra-Lights

2 — 0.2 Milligrams Nicotine or Less

You are Ready to Quit

Bristol Lowest
Cambridge Lowest
Carlton Kings
Carlton 100's

Carlton Ultra
Merit Ultima
Now
Silk Cut Ultra

Store brands, including low-price generic and private-label cigarettes, are all listed in the boxes under the name "Store Brands." Nonfilter store brands have 1.5 milligrams nicotine (Box 15), Full Flavor store brands have 1.1 milligrams nicotine (Box 11), Lights have 0.8 milligrams nicotine (Box 8), and Ultra-Lights have 0.5 milligrams nicotine (Box 5).

Store brands include: Always Save, Austin, Bargain Buy, Bargain King, Beacon, Best Buy, Best Choice, Best Value, Big Money, Black and Yellow, Bonus Value, Cardinal, Cavalier, Citation, Cost Cutter, Director's Choice, Eagle 20's, Econo Buy, Epic, Extra Value, F & L, Famous Value, Federated, 1st Choice, Focus, GPA, Genco, Generic, Gridlock, Highway, Jacks, Kingsport, Marker, Meridian, Money, No Frills, Omni, Pilot, Price Breaker, Price Master, Price Saver, Quality Lights, Quality Smokes, Ralph's, Riviera, Savvy, Scotch Buy, Sebring, Shurfine, Sincerely Yours, Slim Price, Sundance, Tri Brand, Tourney, Upland, Value & Quality, Value Buy, Value Price, Value Sense, Worth, Yours.

Medications

Temporary use of certain medications can take the "edge" off your physical withdrawal symptoms, and double your chances of successful quitting. There are two types of medications: 1) Zyban™ pills; and 2) Nicotine-replacement medications (nicotine skin patches, gum, nasal spray, and inhaler). These medications are discussed briefly below and in more detail in the following sections of this guidebook. Always follow your doctor's directions in using these medications.

Zyban™ pills

Zyban lessens the desire to smoke and reduces withdrawal symptoms. Zyban contains the same medication as the antidepressant Wellbutrin®. However, you do not need to be depressed to benefit from using this medication. Zyban is not safe for everyone—see pages 37 and 38 of this guide.

Nicotine-replacement medications

It may be difficult to accept that nicotine, the very drug that has you "hooked," can help you get "unhooked." The idea is to use "the hair of the dog that bit you" to wean off nicotine.

Some smokers say, "What good is quitting smoking if I still harm my body by using nicotine?" While nicotine can (rarely) be harmful, nicotine is only one of 4000 chemicals and gases in cigarette smoke (see page 83). Nicotine-replacement medicine provides some nicotine while your body clears itself of the other 3999 chemicals in cigarette smoke.

Do not use more than one type of nicotine medicine at a time—you could get too much nicotine. Also, do not smoke, chew tobacco, or use snuff while using any nicotine-replacement medicine.

Which medication should I use?

Any of the medications can help you break free of cigarettes with less discomfort. If you are physically addicted to nicotine (see page 14), you especially should consider using medication to help you quit. With your doctor's help, select the medication that is best for you.

Of the different medications, I generally recommend nicotine skin patches. Many studies have shown that nicotine patches are safe and effective. Nicotine patches are available without a doctor's prescription.

Zyban™ also looks promising, but so far only a few studies of its effects have been completed. Zyban is a good choice if you have tried nicotine patches in the past without success.

It is also possible, with medical supervision, to use nicotine patches and Zyban together. However, there is not yet enough research to tell if the two medications work better together.

The Nicotine Skin Patch

by Dr. Jed Rose

Long before anybody smoked cigarettes, tobacco plants were producing nicotine. In large amounts, nicotine is a poison that discourages insects from eating tobacco leaves. Yet, nicotine is so valued by human beings that they spend many billions of dollars for it.

Why is nicotine so popular, and how does it affect the body and mind? Why does it make sense to use nicotine to help a person give up cigarettes? What is it about a skin patch that makes it such a good tool for kicking smoking addiction?

First, nicotine seems to be so popular because it helps you feel relaxed and calm; interestingly, at the same time it also can pep you up, making it easier to think and concentrate. On top of that, nicotine seems to help you keep trim by reducing appetite and speeding up the rate that you burn calories. Nicotine also may stimulate pleasure pathways in the brain. Finally, a lot of the "taste" of a cigarette, that you may like, is created by the nicotine.

Nicotine also has less desirable effects on the body. It speeds up the heart—after quitting smoking you will be able to measure your pulse and find your heart rate has slowed to normal. Nicotine also constricts blood vessels, causing the temperature of the skin to fall after smoking a cigarette. Nicotine can also raise blood pressure.

Apart from these short-term effects of nicotine, your brain has been bathed in nicotine for so long that this has become your "normal" state. When nicotine levels start to fall after your last cigarette, you feel uncomfortable. After quitting smoking it takes time to get used to being free of nicotine, even though this is more natural.

Why nicotine replacement?

It is much easier to quit smoking by replacing some of the nicotine than by quitting "cold turkey." Later you can gradually give up the replacement nicotine. With nicotine replacement there is less physical withdrawal discomfort, so you can focus on breaking the smoking habit and overcoming your emotional dependence on smoking.

Why a skin patch?

Nicotine is a substance that can dissolve right through the skin and enter the body. The beauty of the nicotine skin patch is that it can release nicotine at a constant rate and maintain a steady level of nicotine in your system.

Temporary use of nicotine skin patches is far less dangerous than continuing to smoke. The patch provides less nicotine than cigarette smoke, and it is free of the cancer-causing chemicals present in cigarette smoke.

What is the patch like?

Nicotine skin patches look like Band-aids®. They come in different sizes, with brand names such as Nicoderm CQ®, Nicotrol®, and Habitrol®. The larger a patch is, the more nicotine it delivers through the skin. Nicoderm CQ, for example, has a large patch that delivers 21 milligrams of nicotine over a 24-hour period ("Step 1"), a medium-size patch that delivers 14 mg. nicotine ("Step 2"), and a small patch that delivers 7 mg. nicotine ("Step 3").

What strength of patch should I use?

Doctors advise most people to start on the strongest patch (15–22 mgs.), and to stay on that strength for at least four weeks before switching to weaker patches. [*Note from Dr. Shipley: If you smoked 25 cigarettes or more, this advice holds even though you switched to low-nicotine cigarettes before starting to use nicotine patches. However, if you smoked between 11 and 24 cigarettes a day and switched to low-nicotine cigarettes, you should start on a middle-strength patch (e.g., Nicoderm CQ Step 2).*] Ask your doctor before using the patch if you smoked less than 11 cigarettes a day, or if you have heart trouble.

How do I use the nicotine skin patch?

Follow the instructions that come with your nicotine patches. Do not start on the patch until you have stopped smoking. Apply a patch once a day (usually when you get up to start your day) to a non-hairy, clean, dry area of your chest, back, hip, or the upper part of your arm. Do not put a patch on skin that is cut or irritated. Press the patch firmly on your skin for about 10 seconds. Make sure it sticks well to your skin, especially around the edges. Water will not harm the patch—you can bathe or swim with the patch on.

Wash your hands after putting on a patch. Nicotine on your hands could get into your eyes or nose and cause irritation.

For some brands of patches (e.g., Nicoderm CQ) you will be instructed to remove the old patch after 24 hours. However, Nicotrol patches are designed to be removed after 16 hours. At the start of your day, put a new patch on a different area of your upper body. Do not reuse a skin area for at least one week.

Although you are to place each patch on a non-hairy area, do not shave the hair off the skin. This could change the amount of nicotine that can enter the body, and make skin irritation more likely. If you have trouble finding a non-hairy area, you may clip the hair short, and then apply a patch.

Remember, nicotine should be kept away from children and pets. That is true of used patches too, because they still contain nicotine. After you put on a new patch, take its opened pouch and place the used patch inside. Throw the pouch in the trash, away from children and pets.

How will I know if I am getting too much or too little nicotine?

For most people, nicotine patches provide just enough nicotine to reduce withdrawal symptoms. However, call your doctor if you believe you are getting either too much nicotine or too little nicotine.

You could be getting too much nicotine if you have a rapid or irregular heartbeat, upset stomach, vomiting, diarrhea, weakness, cold sweat, blurred vision, dizziness, or difficulty falling asleep. The problem of too much nicotine rarely occurs. When it does occur, it is usually in people using the strongest patch (15 to 22 milligrams of nicotine).

If you are not getting enough nicotine from your patch, you could feel very irritable, restless, drowsy, or sad, and have a difficult time concentrating. Other signs of too little nicotine are strong cravings for cigarettes, and difficulty staying asleep. Of course, even with the patch, most people suffer from these symptoms to some extent.

Signs of too little nicotine are most likely to occur in people using a middle-strength patch (10 to 14 milligrams of nicotine), or a low-strength patch (7 milligrams of nicotine). If you think that you are not getting enough nicotine, ask your doctor if you should be using a stronger patch.

How long should I stay on a nicotine patch?

Many people stop using the patch too soon. Most people should stay on nicotine patches for 6–8 weeks, and some people may benefit from using a patch for 10 to 16 weeks or longer. Always follow your doctor's advice about how long to use nicotine patches.

Will I have any problems from wearing a nicotine skin patch?

There are very few side effects that have been reported by people wearing nicotine patches. When you first put on a patch, mild itching, burning or tingling is normal and should go away within an hour. After you remove a patch, your skin under the patch may be somewhat red. This is usually not severe.

If you do have severe skin irritation, such as swelling, a rash or hives, or any other symptoms that concern you, remove the patch and call your doctor. Your doctor may be able to prescribe medicine that will allow you to keep using the patch.

What happens if I smoke while wearing a nicotine patch?

You could get too much nicotine. The best path to success is not to smoke at all after quitting, and to use the patch to make the withdrawal process more bearable.

Will it be easy to quit smoking using the nicotine patch?

When wearing a nicotine patch you are less likely to suffer from several of the major smoking withdrawal symptoms—irritability, anxiety, difficulty concentrating, and drowsiness. Cravings may be less intense and subside sooner with nicotine patches than without.

However, do not expect that your urges to smoke will be erased like magic, especially in situations where you are used to smoking. It is similar to a hospital patient who is fed a sugar solution through a tube in an arm. The patient still misses eating real meals, and smokers still crave cigarettes even when wearing nicotine patches.

Given all the feelings and situations tied to smoking, your urges to smoke will not disappear right away. You will still need the coping skills discussed in the rest of this guide.

Overall, while the patch is not a cure-all, it can double your chance of successful quitting. It is well worth trying.

Nicorette® Nicotine Gum

While Nicorette® nicotine gum is more diffi-cult to use correctly than nicotine patches, you may decide to try Nicorette because you want an oral substitute, or because you had problems using the patch (a skin reaction, for example).

Be sure to follow the instructions that come in Nicorette® packages. Nicorette is available without a doctor's prescription in either 2-milligram or 4-milligram strengths. Use the 2-milligram Nicorette if you smoked less than 25 cigarettes a day. Use 4-milligram Nicorette if you smoked 25 cigarettes a day or more.

Starting on your quit date, chew a piece of Nicorette very slowly until you notice a peppery taste or feel a slight tingling in your mouth (usually after about 15 chews). Then hold ("park") the Nicorette between your gum and cheek. After about one minute, when the peppery taste or tingle is almost gone, chew slowly a few times until the taste or tingle returns, and then again park the piece between your cheek and gum. Use each piece in this way for about thirty minutes.

Use at least 9 to 12 pieces every day (but not more than 24 pieces a day) for your first six weeks off cigarettes. Try to use about one piece every one to two hours that you are awake. After six weeks, gradually reduce your use of Nicorette to one piece every two to four hours. After nine weeks, cut back to one piece every four to eight hours. Stop using Nicorette twelve weeks after your quit date.

Some foods and drinks reduce the effectiveness of Nicorette. Do not eat or drink for 15 minutes before using Nicorette (and while Nicorette is in your mouth). Remember to chew only occasionally—if you chew Nicorette often like regular gum, it can upset your stomach.

Keep used pieces of Nicorette away from children and pets (used pieces still contain nicotine). Ask your doctor before using Nicorette if you are pregnant or nursing.

Also check with your doctor before using Nicorette if you have heart disease, high blood pressure (not controlled by medicine), stomach ulcers, or take insulin for diabetes. If you take prescription medicine for depression or asthma, your doctor may need to adjust the dose of the medicine.

If you have symptoms that might be caused by too much nicotine—nausea, rapid or irregular heartbeat, cold sweat, dizziness—stop using Nicorette and call your doctor. Also, call your doctor if chewing Nicorette causes problems with your mouth, teeth, or jaw. While using Nicorette, do not smoke or use any other nicotine product.

Nicotine Nasal Spray

A squirt of nicotine nasal spray in each nostril gets nicotine into your system much faster than use of the nicotine patch or gum. This quick delivery means fast relief from craving. Some doctors are concerned that this quick "satisfaction" could lead users to become addicted to the spray. Most people, however, are able to stop using the spray without much problem.

The nasal spray may be your best choice in nicotine-replacement products if you are a heavy smoker who has tried nicotine patches in the past without getting much relief. Nicotine nasal spray gives you a tool to use when you are tempted to smoke.

Nicotine nasal spray is available only by prescription. To use the nasal spray, tilt your head back slightly and spray once into each nostril. Do not sniff or inhale while spraying. You will probably notice a hot, peppery feeling in the back of your throat or nose. Stick with it—these side effects will lessen over time.

Starting on your quit date, use the spray at least eight times a day, but not more than five times an hour or 40 times over 24 hours. After six to eight weeks, follow your doctor's instructions for stopping use of the spray.

If you have symptoms that might be due to getting too much nicotine—rapid heartbeat, upset stomach, cold sweat, dizziness—call your doctor. While using the spray, do not smoke or use any other nicotine product.

Nicotrol® Inhaler

The Nicotrol® Inhaler looks like a fat cigarette in a cigarette-holder. Cartridges containing nicotine are placed in the inhaler. When you puff on the inhaler, nicotine passes through the lining of your mouth and throat into your blood stream. Because the nicotine is not absorbed through the lungs, there is no need to inhale deeply. Shallow puffing works best.

Start using the inhaler on your quit date. You will need to take a lot of puffs. It takes eight to ten puffs from an inhaler to get the nicotine provided by one puff on an average cigarette. Follow your doctor's instructions and the directions that come with the inhaler.

In addition to providing a little nicotine with each puff, the inhaler provides a substitute for the habit of smoking. The inhaler may be your best medication choice if you have a strong hand-to-mouth habit but only a mild addiction to nicotine.

The first few times that you use the inhaler, you may notice mild side effects: cough, upset stomach, mouth and throat irritation (the cartridges contain menthol to reduce throat irritation). These side effects should get better with time.

As with other nicotine-replacement medications, if you have symptoms of too much nicotine, call your doctor. Keep the inhaler and nicotine cartridge away from children and pets (even used cartridges contain nicotine).

Zyban™ Pills

Smokers have always wanted a magic pill to make quitting smoking easy. Zyban™ is not that pill. However, Zyban can reduce the desire to smoke and lessen withdrawal symptoms. It is not known why Zyban helps smokers quit, but it could be because Zyban, like smoking, "turns on" some of the pleasure centers in the brain.

Zyban contains the same medication as the antidepressant Wellbutrin®. Many smokers have histories of severe depression—feeling depressed and hopeless every day for two weeks or longer. Zyban may help such smokers keep their mood on an even keel while quitting smoking.

If you do not have problems with depression, you may still want to consider using Zyban to help you quit smoking. Studies have shown that Zyban increases the odds of successful quitting in smokers, including those who do not have histories of depression.

Zyban is available only with a doctor's prescription. If you are planning to use Zyban, make an appointment to see your doctor soon because you will need to start taking Zyban one to two weeks before your quit date.

Your doctor will tell you how to take Zyban. Most smokers are told to take one 150 mg. Zyban pill in the morning for three days. Starting on the fourth day, a second 150 mg. pill is taken in the early evening. From then on, two pills a day are taken. There should be at least eight hours between the morning and evening pills. Generally, Zyban™ use is continued for seven to twelve weeks.

The most common side-effects caused by Zyban are trouble sleeping (30–40% of users) and dry mouth (10% of users). Both of these side effects are usually mild and often disappear after a few weeks of taking Zyban. If you have trouble sleeping, be sure that you are not taking a Zyban pill close to your bedtime.

If your Zyban side effects prove to be more than you want to tolerate, ask your doctor if you can reduce your dose of Zyban to one pill each morning. One study found that a single 150 mg Zyban pill each day worked about as well as two pills a day (Hurt, et. al, *The New England Journal of Medicine*, Volume 337). The one pill option also saves money.

Zyban is not safe for everyone. There is a risk of seizures in some people. You should not take Zyban if you: have a seizure disorder, are already taking the antidepressant Wellbutrin®, have ever had an eating disorder (bulimia or anorexia nervosa), or have recently taken anti-depressant medications known as MAO inhibitors (Marplan, Nardil, Parnate). Zyban is not recommended for women who are pregnant or breast-feeding.

Should You Reduce Caffeine?

Many smokers consume a lot of caffeine. Caffeine is a stimulant found in coffee, tea, cola, chocolate, and some medications. Smokers clear caffeine from their bodies faster than do non-smokers. That is one reason smokers drink so much coffee and cola.

Use the Caffeine Count table on the following pages to see how much caffeine you are taking in. If you are taking in more than 400 milligrams a day (about four cups of coffee), on your quit date cut back your caffeine intake by about one third. A smoker who drinks six cups of coffee a day, on the quit date would cut back to four cups a day.

After you stop smoking, caffeine will stay in your body longer. The one-third reduction in caffeine intake will keep the level of caffeine in your body about the same as when you were a smoker.

Do not cut back too much—caffeine is addictive. If you abruptly swear off most caffeine, you could suffer withdrawal symptoms such as headaches, irritability, and sleepiness. You do not need these symptoms when you are quitting smoking.

The Caffeine Count

Substance	Milligrams of Caffeine
COFFEE and TEA	
Espresso (2 oz.)	120
Regular coffee, brewed (6 oz.)	100
Instant coffee (6 oz.)	60
Brewed Tea (6 oz.)	50
Fruitopia Iced Tea (16 oz.)	22
DRINKS, 12 oz.	
Java Juice	90
Jolt Cola	72
Josta, Nehi Maxxvm Cola	70
Krank20 water; Java Water	70
XTC Juice	70
Mountain Dew	55
Mello Yello; Surge	51
Coca-Cola; Diet Coke	45
RC Cola; Diet RC Cola	46
Water Joe	46
Dr. Pepper; Mr. Pibb	41
Pepsi-Cola; Diet Pepsi	37
A&W Cream Soda	35

MEDICATIONS

No Doz - 2 tablets	200
Vivarin - 1 tablet	200
Excedrin - 2 tablets	130
Actamin Super - 2 tablets	130
Cafergot - 1 tablet	100
Vanquish - 2 tablets	66
Anacin - 2 tablets	65
Midol - 2 tablets	65
Migrol - 1 tablet	50
Fiorinal - 1 tablet	40
Dristan - 2 tablets	32
Darvon Compound - 1 tablet	32
Coryban-D - 1 tablet	30
Sinarest - 1 tablet	30
Norgesic - 1 tablet	30

CHOCOLATE

Baking chocolate (1 oz.)	35
Chocolate candy bar, small	15-25
Cocoa drink (6 oz.)	5-20
Chocolate milk (8 oz.)	5

Let Family and Friends Help

Many people pride themselves on being self-reliant, independent, and strong-willed. They try to quit smoking by toughing it out alone, without the support of others. Some people do not even tell others that they are trying to quit. This is not quitting smart. People who arrange a support system for their quitting efforts are more likely to succeed, and they succeed with greater comfort.

Ask for the support of several family members and friends. You will want a supportive person at home, at work, and in social situations. Tell these people of your plans to quit, ask for their support, and discuss with them how they can help you. For example, you might ask them to:

- Read this guide so they understand your quitting program.

- Go with you on smoke-free activities (a walk, a movie).

- Help talk you through urges.

- Praise you for not smoking.

- Give you rewards (hugs, cards, flowers).

- Not remind you of past difficulties in quitting.

- Be tolerant of your withdrawal symptoms (irritability, nervousness).

- Not nag or attempt to police you.

- Remind you that withdrawal symptoms will pass.

- Point out positive changes (you look healthier, breathe easier).

- Express confidence in your ability to remain a nonsmoker.

- Realize that you can use special support for a full year.

Review this list with your support people so you can plan the best support strategy. Do not be shy about doing this. Your family and friends want you alive and well, and will be pleased when you request their help.

Be sure to tell your family and friends how much you appreciate their support. A few weeks after your quit date, send each person a thank you note or a small gift.

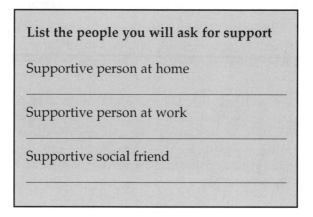

List the people you will ask for support

Supportive person at home

_____

Supportive person at work

_____

Supportive social friend

_____

Stop the Debate

George quit smoking but suffered much longer than most people. Several weeks after quitting, he was still irritable and anxious, and had lots of urges for a cigarette. With each urge, he debated: "Should I smoke or not? Maybe I could have just one."

Then something happened. His best buddy, a smoker, was diagnosed as having lung cancer. This hit George very hard. Cigarettes were killing his best friend. George decided—*really decided*—that he would never smoke again, that he was a nonsmoker no matter what! Most of the withdrawal symptoms disappeared. He suffered no more irritability, no more "nerves," and he had few urges to smoke. Why?

Once George really decided that, no matter what, he would never smoke again, the internal debate ended. It was this constant debate, the back and forth thoughts about whether or not to have a cigarette, that caused his long suffering.

Once you really decide you are a nonsmoker, urges are not relevant. You no longer have to think about cigarettes all the time, and your mind can go on to more pleasant things.

If you have not yet made a firm decision to quit for good, think it through one last time. It may not be an easy decision. If despite mixed feelings, you decide that you want most to quit, make your decision and do not debate it further. When you make a firm decision to quit, you will be surprised at how easy quitting can be.

Avoid Smoking Temptations

Before you quit, it is smart to "smoke-proof" your home, car, and workplace. Most important is reducing, or getting rid of, things that serve as triggers for smoking.

Destroy all your cigarettes. Just before your quit date, destroy all your cigarettes. The sight and smell of cigarettes will only tempt you. Be sure you search out every last cigarette and cigarette butt and destroy them completely! Also, remove ash trays and lighters.

Avoid smokers. For your first few weeks as a nonsmoker, avoid being around people who are smoking. Do not schedule lunch dates or social outings with smokers during this risky time. Ask close friends and relatives not to smoke around you.

For the long term, make a point of getting to know your nonsmoking friends better. By spending more time with your nonsmoking friends, you will be more likely to remain free of cigarettes.

Avoid smoky places. Smoky places tend to serve as triggers for smoking. Try to avoid smoking-allowed bars, restaurants, bowling alleys, coffee-break areas, and parties where people may be smoking. Even places in your own home or office that you associate with cigarettes, such as your favorite "smoking chair," should be avoided for a time.

Select Your Quit Date

If you have not already done so, now is the time to select your quit date. This will be your first day of freedom from cigarettes. Your quit date should be one to three weeks in the future to allow time to:

- Arrange for the support of family and friends.

- Reduce your addiction to nicotine by switching to cigarette brands that have less nicotine.

- Talk to your doctor about use of medications to help you quit. Use of a nicotine-replacement product begins on your quit date. If you decide to use Zyban™, you will need to start taking the pills at least one week prior to your quit date.

- Prepare urge-control methods by studying the *Quitting* chapter of this guide.

- Destroy all your cigarettes, and remove ashtrays (just before your quit date).

If possible, select a quit date that will not be stressful, perhaps a Saturday or a vacation day. *Write your quit date on the next page* and circle it on your calendar. Stick to your quit date.

QUIT SMART™

Stop Smoking Contract

I will quit smoking on

_____
(date)

and do all I can to stay
free of cigarettes

_____
Your signature

_____
Date

CHAPTER 2
Quitting

Hats off to you for getting this far, and for devoting the time and energy to plan ahead for successful quitting. You are now ready to quit.

You have a lot of tools to help you succeed. On your quit date you will start listening to your hypnosis tape, and start using your Better Quit® cigarette substitute. You may also begin using the nicotine patch, gum, nasal spray, or inhaler on your quit date. If you are taking Zyban™ pills, you will continue to do so.

In this chapter, you will learn to keep withdrawal symptoms in perspective and *actively do things to cope*. You will learn to relax, to use "tricks" that help to control cigarette urges, and to use your thoughts to make nonsmoking easier.

Keep using the methods you have already learned: call on your family and friends for support, avoid people who smoke and places where smoking occurs, and refer often to your list of reasons for quitting.

The quitting phase lasts about a week. Then your task turns to remaining a nonsmoker. Look ahead at Chapter 3, *Remaining a Nonsmoker,* so you will be prepared for this challenge.

Learn to Relax

Most of us suffer to some degree from tension and tension-related symptoms such as upset stomach, headaches, difficulty sleeping, and tiredness. Withdrawal from cigarettes may produce a temporary increase in feelings of tension. By practicing the relaxation methods discussed below, you will learn to relax while keeping your mind clear and sharp.

Take a breather. Much of the relaxation you get from smoking a cigarette is due to pausing and taking several slow deep breaths. Try "taking a breather." Take a slow breath, drawing the air deep into your belly; hold it a few seconds, and then exhale slowly as you let your muscles relax and say to yourself the word "calm" or "relax." Repeat this several times. Practice taking two or three relaxing deep breaths twenty times a day.

Use daily events to remind you to take breathers. For example, take a breather when you hang up the phone, during television ads, when you feel annoyed, and whenever you can use a relaxing break. Also, take a breather if you have an urge for a cigarette. The slow deep breaths will relieve your craving for a cigarette, and leave you more relaxed and in control.

Take vitamins. Stress can rob you of vitamins and minerals. If your doctor does not object, take multivitamins.

Add physical activity. Take a daily walk. The goal is to add pleasant activities to your day. Do not overdo it—starting a difficult exercise program can add stress rather than reduce it.

Solve sleep problems. If you have trouble sleeping, be sure you are not drinking something with caffeine (coffee, tea, or cola) within six hours of bed time. Also, avoid naps. Your sleep should improve within a week or two after quitting. As a nonsmoker, you may need less sleep than you did as a smoker. For example, you might be able to stay up 15 minutes later before going to bed.

If you are wearing a nicotine skin patch at night and have difficulty falling asleep or have overly vivid dreams, this could be a side-effect of the patch. Your doctor may recommend removing the patch at bedtime, or changing to a lower-strength patch. The medication Zyban™ can also disrupt sleep—call your doctor if this is a problem.

Use physical methods to relax. Hot baths, massage, stretching exercises, a hot-water bottle, and relaxing music are all calming. Each of these can be used as often as you wish and require no outside help (even massage can be self-massage).

Remember, you will soon feel better. Within six months of breaking free from cigarettes, most exsmokers report feeling more relaxed and happy than they felt while smoking.

Use Hypnosis

Hypnosis is simply relaxation with focused attention. It is a way to use the full power of your mind to reach your goal of becoming a nonsmoker. There is no magic; you remain in control.

Start using the *QuitSmart Hypnosis* audio tape on your quit date. The deep voice of Robert Conroy will help you relax and enjoy life as a nonsmoker. If you do not have this tape, see the order form on the last page of this guide. A Spanish version of this tape is also available.

Side One of the tape, *Quitting*, eases you through your first few weeks of freedom from cigarettes. The suggestions on the tape help you relax and enjoy healthy pleasures, as you avoid unwanted weight gain or other negative side effects.

Side Two, *Remaining a Nonsmoker*, helps to instill the feelings of inner calm and strength that are most helpful in staying free of cigarettes for a lifetime.

What is hypnosis?
Hypnosis is relaxation with focused attention. You have probably been in a hypnotic state while watching a good movie or listening to music. Whenever you relax and become so focused on one thing that you are not easily distracted, you are using the powerful state of mind called hypnosis.

How should I use the hypnosis tape?

Start using the tape on your quit date. Pick a time and place where you will not be disturbed for at least 15 minutes. Turn the lights down, get comfortable in a chair, sofa, or bed that supports all parts of your body. Start the tape and relax.

How often should I listen to the tape?

The more times you listen to the tape, the better. Start listening to Side One, *Quitting*, on your quit date. Listen at least twice daily during your first week off cigarettes. The next week, listen to Side One once daily, and listen to Side Two, *Remaining a Nonsmoker*, once a day. After that, listen to Side One or Two as often as you want or need to, listening most often to the side you find more relaxing and helpful.

How will I know if I was in a hypnotic state?

You will simply feel relaxed, your hands may feel heavy and warm, or they may tingle. You may also notice some time distortion, with the tape seeming to play for more or less time than it actually requires. In any case, you do not need to be in a deeply hypnotized state to benefit from the tape.

Should I concentrate hard and try to remember everything on the tape?

No. Just relax and let the voice on the tape "be there" without trying to concentrate on every word. Listen to the voice but do not worry about the words too much.

What if I get stuck in hypnosis and can't get out?

You cannot get stuck in the hypnotic state. The hypnotic state is between sleep and wakefulness; you pass through this state when you fall asleep and again when you wake up. If you are tired when you listen to the tape, you could fall asleep. You would wake up as you normally do—when you are rested, or when there is a noise or someone calls your name.

Can I use the tape at night to help me fall asleep?

Yes, but the suggestions on the tape are most helpful if you are in the hypnotic state between sleep and wakefulness. Therefore, it is best to listen to the tape and then allow yourself to go to sleep. The instructions at the end of Side Two may help—they tell you to return to your normal waking state, "unless you have decided to use this tape to fall asleep."

Is it alright to listen to the tape while driving?

No. Since hypnosis can make you sleepy, **do not listen while driving or using machines**.

Will the tape benefit me in any way in addition to helping me break free from cigarettes?

It will help you to relax more quickly and completely. This can reduce stress symptoms such as headaches, upset stomach, irritability, and sleep problems.

Better Quit®
Cigarette Substitute

New exsmokers are like newcomers to a nudist colony—they don't know what to do with their hands. The Better Quit® Cigarette Substitute gives you something to do with your hands and mouth. It looks and feels like a real cigarette. The Better Quit® Substitute also reminds you to take deep, relaxing breaths—just like you did when you smoked cigarettes. (To order Better Quit, see page 94.)

You smoked primarily to get a "hit" of nicotine to your brain. The look and feel of a cigarette became pleasurable because you associated the cigarette with this "hit" of nicotine. Better Quit will help you break this association. Since Better Quit has no nicotine, use of Better Quit gradually lessens the pleasure associated with the look and feel of a cigarette.

Begin using Better Quit on your quit date. Adjust the air flow to your liking by sliding the filter in or out. Take deep draws of fresh air, and enjoy relaxing. Use the carrying tube to keep Better Quit clean and handy.

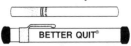

Carry Better Quit in your pocket or purse and use it whenever you are tempted to smoke. Gradually, the power of these situations to tempt you will decrease. When Better Quit no longer gives you pleasure, stop regular use. However, continue to carry Better Quit with you to help deal with rare urges for a cigarette.

Thinking Makes It So

The human mind has the power to create feelings out of thin air. For example, you may be able to create hunger by thinking about a juicy steak, or sleepiness by imagining a yawn coming on. This power of the mind can be used in three ways to help you stay free from cigarettes. You can use your thoughts and images to create a nonsmoking self-image, to control cigarette urges, and to keep life's hassles in perspective.

Create a nonsmoking self-image. A person's self-image has a powerful effect on behavior. When you think of yourself as a nonsmoker, you will behave as a nonsmoker. You will, for example, sit in the nonsmoking section of restaurants. Cigarette ads will not tempt you because you are a nonsmoker. If you feel bored or anxious, you will not interpret those feelings as an urge for a cigarette because nonsmokers do not have such urges.

The effect of self-image on behavior is well known in sports. Greg Louganis became a world champion diver, in part, by thinking of himself as a great diver and by imagining himself performing each dive perfectly. The author of this guide used to improve his tennis game by imagining that he was Jimmy Connors. As "Jimmy," he was a stronger, more confident tennis player.

You are what you believe. Believing you are a permanent nonsmoker who is calm and happy will naturally lead to that outcome. Do not make the mistake of trying to break your cigarette addiction while a part of you is still thinking of yourself as a smoker. See smoking as something that you did a long time ago; you were a different person then. Now you are a nonsmoker.

Control cigarette urges. Most urges for a cigarette can be controlled by simply focusing your thoughts elsewhere. Focusing your thoughts on an urge to smoke is like focusing on an itchy nose. It will drive you crazy. Instead, turn your thoughts to something pleasant, like a walk on the beach.

Keep life's hassles in perspective. You have probably known people who get very upset with the least little mishap, and other people who handle a crisis calmly. The ability to "roll with the punches" will be important during your first few weeks without cigarettes.

The key to maintaining perspective on life's hassles is to realize that the way you think about a situation will determine your feelings about it. For example, when caught in a traffic jam, you can make yourself very angry by thinking, "I'll never be on time; this is awful," or relatively calm by thinking, "This is a chance to 'take a breather' and enjoy the radio."

Your thoughts can make quitting smoking either difficult or relatively easy. Quitting will be difficult if you tell yourself that withdrawal symptoms are terrible, and that you will not succeed. Instead, tell yourself that you accept some discomfort, and that you are adding freedom and self-control to your life. With positive thinking, quitting can be surprisingly easy and fulfilling.

Shakespeare wrote, "There is nothing either good or bad, but thinking makes it so." (*Hamlet*, Act II, Scene 2.) Using your thoughts wisely will help you stay calm and avoid making "mountains out of molehills."

Overcome Withdrawal Symptoms

At first the challenge of breaking free of cigarettes is getting through physical withdrawal. Your body is used to getting nicotine in hundreds of daily puffs. The use of brand switching and medication will reduce any discomfort, but you may briefly experience increases in some of the following symptoms:

- frustration, irritability, anger
- sadness, depression
- difficulty sleeping
- anxiety
- restlessness
- difficulty concentrating
- cravings for tobacco
- hunger
- daytime sleepiness
- lightheadedness, dizziness
- tingling or numbness in arms and legs
- constipation or diarrhea
- sweating
- coughing

Each person has different symptoms. For example, some people feel tense, while others feel drowsy. Many people have little discomfort. Any symptoms you have are temporary and are a sign that your body is healing itself.

Remember:

Withdrawal symptoms are temporary; they will soon pass. Symptoms generally peak during the first three to six days, and mostly disappear within two to four weeks. Soon after that, as a nonsmoker, you will be healthier and calmer than you were as a smoker.

Urges are short-lived. It may seem that an urge lasts forever, but actually an urge peaks and subsides within three to five minutes. If you interrupt an urge with a coping method (deep breaths, pleasant thoughts), you will conquer it even sooner.

Withdrawal symptoms are a sign that your body is healing itself.

- "Tingling" in your arms and legs results from better blood flow.

- Feeling dizzy or lightheaded sometimes occurs as your brain gets more oxygen than it is used to.

- Coughing may increase for a few days as your lung's hair-like cilia, no longer paralyzed by tobacco smoke, work overtime to remove "tar" from your lungs.

- You may sweat more as chemicals from tobacco smoke are flushed out of your body through the skin's pores.

Use coping methods. Take deep, relaxing breaths, use the Better Quit® substitute, listen to your hypnosis tape, and drink plenty of water.

Consider increasing nicotine medication. If you are using a nicotine-replacement product, and are still having severe withdrawal symptoms, ask your doctor if you should use a higher dose of nicotine.

Notice positive changes. It is important to look for the first signs of physical and mental improvement. After a few days to a week of freedom from cigarettes, you will discover many of the following positive changes:

- You can walk farther without feeling winded.
- Your hands and feet are warmer due to improved blood flow.
- Your skin looks rosier, healthier.
- You breathe more easily.
- You have more energy.
- Your sleep improves.
- Your sinuses clear.
- Your teeth and fingers are cleaner.
- Your pulse rate drops as your heart's job becomes easier.
- Your senses of smell and taste improve.
- You have a sense of rebirth and pride in your success.

After being free of cigarettes for several days, begin keeping a list of the positive changes you notice.

_____

_____

_____

_____

_____

_____

_____

_____

_____

_____

_____

_____

_____

Habit Buster Tips

The smoking habit may be strong, but it is also dumb—you can outsmart it! Small changes in your habits can reduce your urges to smoke. Try the following:

- **Leave the table when you finish eating.** Brush your teeth or take a walk. This will help you stop associating finishing a meal with a cigarette.

- **Change habits that you associate with smoking**. If you smoked while talking on the phone, talk in a different room, hold the phone in the other hand, or sit in a different chair. If you usually smoked while sitting in your favorite chair, avoid that "smoking chair" for a while.

- **Change your work breaks**. For most smokers, a cigarette and a work break go together. So, change your break routine—go to a different location (smoke free), and take deep relaxing breaths or use oral substitutes.

- **Keep busy**. Take up a hobby, go to the movies, go for a walk, work around the house, call or visit friends, write letters, or read a book.

- **Increase your physical activity**. Walk daily, or take up an active hobby. The next time you need a pick-me-up, try some jumping jacks or a walk in the fresh air.

- **Keep your hands and mouth busy**. Use the Better Quit® cigarette substitute. You may also want to try sugarless mints or gum, toothpicks, cinnamon sticks, carrot and celery sticks, crushed ice and water.

Coping Methods to Remember

1. **Drink plenty of fluids**. Drink lots of water and other beverages (at least eight glasses a day) to help flush the cigarette poisons from your body.

2. **Avoid swings in blood sugar**. Eat regular meals with lots of fruits, vegetables, and grains. Avoid foods that contain a lot of sugar.

3. **Relax**. "Take a breather" many times a day and whenever you have an urge to smoke.

4. **Remind yourself that urges will pass**. An urge passes within three to five minutes—you can wait it out.

5. **Think about what you will buy**. Plan how you will spend the money no longer wasted on cigarettes and medical bills.

6. **Ask friends and relatives for help**. Tell them you are quitting and how they can help.

7. **Praise yourself**. Think often of your pride at resisting cigarettes. Mentally pat yourself on the back each time you outsmart an urge.

8. **Note your improvements**. For example, if your sense of smell has improved or you have more "wind," focus your thoughts on these positive changes.

9. **Express your frustrations and anger**. Gently stick up for your rights, or pound a pillow, or take a walk. Do something with your frustrations; do not let them do something to you by serving as an excuse for a cigarette.

10. **Phone for help**. Call the National Cancer Information Service for free quitting advice: 1-800-422-6237. If you are using a nicotine-replacement product or Zyban™, call the phone support numbers listed in the instructions that come with these medications.

11. **Feel proud**. When you see someone smoking, feel proud that you no longer have such a harmful addiction. Let yourself feel a bit superior and smug.

CHAPTER 3
Remaining a Nonsmoker

Congratulations! You are over the worst. From here on, urges become less frequent. Your task now turns to staying a nonsmoker over the long haul. This chapter will prepare you to overcome situations that often lead new exsmokers to "fall off the wagon."

Relapse is most common during periods of negative emotions (anger, frustration, anxiety, or depression). To keep your mood on an even keel, you will learn to increase the positives in your life and decrease the negatives. Continued use of your relaxation skills ("taking a breather," daily walks) and use of medication will also help control negative emotions.

Relapse occurs for some people when others pressure them to "have just one." You will learn firm responses to such smoking come-ons. Likewise, you may be tempted by your own thoughts ("I need a cigarette to handle this crisis"), and firm responses are needed here, too. You will also learn the folly of thinking you can smoke "just one."

Finally, weight gain, which may or may not be due to quitting smoking, often serves as an excuse for relapse. Instead, you will learn to control your weight by using methods similar to those you used to overcome smoking.

Accentuate the Positive

Now that you have given up the pleasure of smoking, it is important to increase other pleasures in your daily life. In the 1944 movie, "Here Come The Waves," Bing Crosby sang:

> *"You've got to Accentuate The Positive*
> *Eliminate The Negative*
> *Latch on to The Affirmative*
> *Don't mess around with Mister Inbetween."*
>
> LYRICS BY JOHNNY MERCER

If you have too many negatives in your day, and not enough positives, you can get frustrated and depressed. It can be tempting to smoke in order to feel better.

Instead, add some positives: appreciate the little things in life such as a beautiful sunset, do something each day that gives you pleasure, buy gifts for yourself, and think pleasant thoughts. Also, be on the lookout for negatives you can eliminate.

Many new exsmokers fail to act on these ideas because they have trouble being nice to themselves; but so much depends on your taking action—your happiness, the happiness of those around you, and your productivity.

Get some ideas from the following lists of ways other exsmokers have added positives and eliminated negatives. Then make your own lists of positives you will accentuate, and negatives you will eliminate.

Positives added

- Karen took pleasant walks after dinner.

- Jill treated herself to a bubble bath.

- Jack started getting a massage each week.

- Steve paused for slow deep breaths.

- Sue bought a flower every week.

- Rod bought several compact discs.

- Bert focused on life's little pleasures.

Little Things

Most of us miss out
on life's big prizes.
The Pulitzer. The Nobel. Oscars. Tonys. Emmys.
But we're all eligible for
life's small pleasures.
A pat on the back.
A kiss
behind the ear.
A four-pound bass. A full moon.
An empty parking space.
A crackling fire. A great meal. A glorious sunset.
Hot soup.
Cold beer.
Don't fret about copping life's grand awards.
Enjoy its tiny delights.
There are plenty for all of us.

—Anonymous

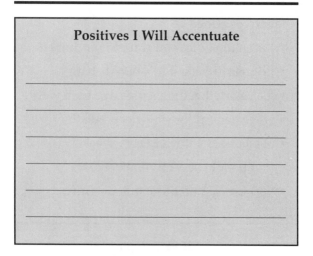

Positives I Will Accentuate

_____

_____

_____

_____

_____

_____

Negatives eliminated

- Mary resigned from a committee that she disliked.

- Elaine got rid of the hassle of phone calls during the family dinner by taking the phone off the hook.

- Sam decided to stop feeling guilty for wanting some time to himself.

- Ron traded his least favorite chore—loading the dishwasher—for walking the dog, a pleasant way of increasing exercise.

- Jackie decided to take some time off work to do things she enjoys.

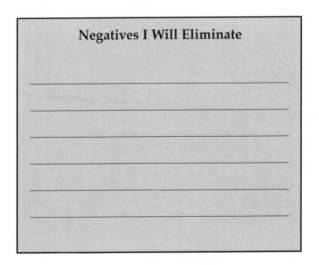

Negatives I Will Eliminate

Rebuff Smoking Come-ons

Most people will try to help you stay free of cigarettes, but a few may try to tempt you to smoke again. This can happen because your success threatens them or because they are impatient with your temporary irritability or other withdrawal symptoms. Either way, it pays to prepare yourself to stand up for your decision to remain a nonsmoker.

Smoking Come-on	Possible Response
"Have a cigarette, just one won't hurt."	"No, it's stupid to tempt fate. I'm glad to be a nonsmoker."
"You're so irritable; have a cigarette."	"I may be irritable, but I'm not crazy. Please don't offer me a cigarette."
"We're having such a good time; join me in a cigarette."	"I don't smoke any-more. Why don't you join me for a walk?"
"Congratulations on a good job. You deserve a cigarette."	"I don't smoke, but I'll have a soft drink."
"Have a cigarette; you're going to die sooner or later anyway."	"No thanks, I'd prefer later."

SMOKING COME-ONS...

Control the Enemy Within

As you reviewed the smoking come-ons, you may have realized that you have used some of these come-ons against yourself. Perhaps you told yourself "have just one" or "have a cigarette to calm your irritability" or "you deserve a cigarette."

When this happens, be just as forceful with yourself as you will be if somebody else goes against your decision to be free of cigarettes. Look back over the come-ons on page 74 and put a check mark by any that you have used on yourself.

Listed below are other common self come-ons and possible responses.

Self Come-on	Possible Response
Nostalgia: "Smoking was so great with coffee."	"Maybe, but there were also times cigarettes tasted bad."
Crisis: "I can't handle this without a cigarette."	"No, a cigarette only makes me feel more defeated. I'll take a few deep breaths and handle this."
Anger: "I'll show that so-and-so; I'll smoke a cigarette."	"I'll stick up for myself *and* stick by *my* decision to be a nonsmoker."
Defeatism: "Since I'm a jerk anyway, I may as well smoke."	"Nobody's perfect, but I'm proud that I quit smoking."

Stay on the Wagon

Did you know that among exsmokers who have "just one" cigarette, nine out of ten soon return to regular smoking? After two cigarettes, the odds are even worse. Some exsmokers think they can beat the odds—but why try? Other exsmokers want to smoke "just one" to prove how strong they are. However, it shows more strength to resist temptation.

Exsmokers who have one cigarette feel guilty and discouraged. They think of themselves as smokers. Believing that the battle is already lost, they go back to regular smoking ("I already blew it, so I might as well smoke another.")

You have made a wise decision to quit smoking and have invested lots of time and energy to become a nonsmoker. It only makes sense now to protect your investment by never allowing yourself "just one."

Dwight Eisenhower quit smoking in 1949 after he had a (probable) heart attack. It wasn't easy to quit—he had been a four-pack-a-day smoker. At a 1957 press conference, President Eisenhower said, "I don't know whether I will start smoking but I will never stop again."

By never having "just one," you will never again have to quit smoking. Underscore your determination to stay completely free of cigarettes by signing the contract below.

QUIT SMART™

No Smoking Contract

I pledge to remain totally free of cigarettes.

_____
Your signature

_____
Date

Weight Control

Weight gain is a prime reason some people give for going back to smoking. Four out of five people who quit smoking gain some weight.

Without the stimulation of nicotine, the body uses fewer calories. Despite needing fewer calories, the new exsmoker may eat more because food tastes better, and because eating serves as an oral substitute for smoking.

Try to accept a few added pounds as a trade off for feeling better and living longer. You need not look like the thin models in cigarette ads.

If you gain more than five pounds, devise a weight control strategy. However, if you try to lose weight quickly or too soon after quitting smoking, you are likely to return to smoking. Avoid starvation diets, fad diets, and diet pills. Eat three nutritious meals a day while limiting fattening foods.

It is a good idea, however, to allow for an occasional snack or sweet by cutting back calories elsewhere. If you entirely forbid certain foods that you desire, these foods can become so tempting that it is only a matter of time before you overeat (or go back to smoking).

Controlling weight is similar to controlling smoking. Many of the methods that you have found helpful in staying off cigarettes can help you control your weight.

- **Relax**. "Take a breather" to relax and control the urge to overeat.

- **Stay physically active**. A daily walk reduces stress, lessens hunger, and burns calories.

- **Avoid overeating temptations**. Do not keep fattening foods in the house. Grocery shop only when you are not hungry.

- **Think of yourself as a healthy eater**. Remember "thinking makes it so." Think of yourself as a person who is very selective about what you eat, a "picky" eater who always leaves some food on your plate.

- **Control the enemy within**. Look back at the section "Control the Enemy Within" and plan how you will respond to similar thoughts that tempt you to go off your weight control diet.

- **Use self-rewards**. When you eat sensibly, reward yourself. Avoid depression and anger by increasing the positives in your life and decreasing the negatives.

- **Listen to your hypnosis tape**. Side One of the tape includes suggestions to help control weight.

If you gain weight, do not go back to smoking. Most people who go back to cigarettes do not lose much weight. Accept a small weight gain as a normal part of gaining your freedom from cigarettes. For a large weight gain, "LoseSmart" by tackling that problem much the same as you did the smoking problem.

Dangers of Smoking

Often smokers avoid learning all the harmful effects of cigarettes because these effects are so frightening. However, now that you are free of cigarettes, knowing the dangers of smoking will strengthen your resolve to remain a nonsmoker.

Physical problems of smokers

- Heart disease

- Lung cancer

- Cancers of the mouth, larynx, esophagus, colon, bladder, kidney, pancreas, stomach, breast, skin, and reproductive organs

- Emphysema and bronchitis

- Stomach ulcers

- Stroke (due to hardening or clogging of blood vessels in the brain)

- Bone calcium loss (osteoporosis)

- Facial wrinkles (due to poor blood flow to the skin, the drying effects of smoke, and puckering the lips)

- Headaches

- Eye cataracts and glaucoma

- Low sex drive, male sexual impotence, and decreased fertility.

- Early onset of menopause

- High blood pressure

- Women who smoke while pregnant are more likely to have babies that do not weigh enough to be healthy.

- Low back pain

- Shortness of breath

- Colds, coughs, and sore throats

Health effects on loved ones

Second-hand smoke exposure can be dangerous. Second-hand smoke can cause lung cancer in nonsmokers, and it increases the chance that a nonsmoker will die from heart disease.

Children who live with smokers are twice as likely to suffer from poor health as are children not exposed to smoke. Children of smokers are more likely to suffer from colds, sore throats, asthma, chronic ear infections, bronchitis, and pneumonia.

Some of the 4000 chemicals smokers inhale

Acetaldehyde, acetone, aceturitrile, acrolein, acrylonitrile, ammonia, **arsenic**, benzene, butylamine, carbon monoxide, carbon dioxide, cresols, crotononitrile, **DDT**, dimethylamine, endrin, ethylamine, formaldehyde, furfural hydroquinone, **hydrogen cyanide** (used in the gas chamber), hydrogen sulfide, methacrolein, methyl alcohol, methylamine, nickel compounds, nicotine, nitric oxide, nitrogen dioxide, phenol, **polonium-210 (radioactive)**, pyridine, "tar" (burned plant resins).

Benefits of Nonsmoking

Now that you are a nonsmoker, it is important to focus on the many benefits you will enjoy. You will save money, you will feel better, and more.

You will save lots of money. The cost of cigarettes is increasing every year. Assuming cigarettes cost $2.50 a pack, if you were a two-pack-a-day smoker, you will save $1,825 a year—that is $36,500 over the next 20 years! What can you buy with that?

Smart exsmokers spend the money they save on things they enjoy. By giving yourself nice things, you increase your chances of remaining a nonsmoker.

As an exsmoker, you also save money by being much less likely than a smoker to suffer a serious illness. On average, a thirty-nine year-old man who breaks a two-pack-a-day cigarette addiction will save $75,000 in medical costs, and in earnings and productivity not lost due to illness.

You may also be able to save money on your insurance premiums. Reduced rates are offered by many companies to nonsmokers on insurance for health, life, car, and house. Smokers pay higher house insurance premiums because they tend to burn their houses down. They pay more for car insurance because they have more accidents, perhaps due to fumbling for cigarettes rather than watching the road.

You feel better. You have more energy, you look better, your heart rate is lower, your hands and feet are warmer due to improved blood flow, and you are proud of getting free of cigarettes.

Listed below are benefits noted by ex-smokers just a few weeks after breaking free from cigarettes.

How many of these benefits are you enjoying?

- I feel in control of my life for the first time in fifteen years.
- I like not burning holes in my clothes and furniture.
- I've inspired others to quit.
- I don't believe how calm I am.
- I feel more poised in social situations.
- Now I am a good model for my kids.
- Glad to know that past failures were due to lack of knowledge, not lack of willpower.
- I feel great!
- I have so much more time.
- It's amazing how much I get done now that I have two hands.
- I enjoy having more money to spend on me.
- No more sinus headaches—it's wonderful.
- My skin is healthy pink instead of ash gray.

- Sour stomach is completely gone.
- Now I can play two sets of tennis without fading from lack of lung power.
- The house is cleaner, and smells fresher.
- My sex drive picked up; I feel ten years younger.
- I eat slower and enjoy my food—don't rush through the meal to get a cigarette.
- I enjoyed the half-time show at a basketball game while the addicts rushed out for a cigarette.
- I feel more attractive—actually, I am more attractive.
- I no longer hide my anger in a cloud of smoke.
- I feel self-confident.
- I'm starting to take better care of myself in other ways.
- I don't have to empty dirty ashtrays ever again.
- I no longer have to feel embarrassed about being a smoker.
- I can feel smug when I see tobacco ads.
- No more tobacco film on my car windows.
- I'm keeping things in better perspective; I now see little hassles as little hassles.
- I no longer have to make excuses about why I'm still smoking.

- No more angry looks from people whose air is being polluted.
- Proud that I quit just for me.
- It's great not to worry about starting an accidental fire.
- I don't have to worry about my smoke hurting others.
- I sleep better and wake up refreshed.
- My heart stopped skipping beats.
- My lover tells me I'm more "kissable."
- I climbed the stairs to the third floor and could still talk.
- I feel so strong and competent.
- My husband told me he liked my new perfume—the same one I generally wear but without the smoke smell.
- I love smelling flowers now.
- I'm the envy of the office—they all want to quit now.
- I no longer feel like a social outcast.
- I got my teeth cleaned and they stayed clean.
- I smile more.
- Don't have to worry about always having available a cigarette, lighter, and ashtray.
- I love saying, "I'm a nonsmoker."
- I seem to have more time to enjoy myself.

- I haven't had a cold in months.
- That hacking smoker's cough is gone.
- My hair no longer smells like stale smoke.
- I look forward to living a longer life.
- I don't need as much sleep as I used to.
- I feel good about taking better care of my body.
- I no longer worry about a heart attack.
- I enjoy being the resident expert at work on how to quit smoking.
- Nasal passages are clear—I can breathe.
- The pain in my chest is gone.
- No longer cough up black stuff.
- My ulcer calmed down.
- I don't have to hide behind a cigarette anymore.
- I can be close to people without worrying about smoker's breath.
- No longer have to frantically read the signs to see if it's O.K. to smoke.
- New man I met told me he would never date a smoker.
- Glad I "QuitSmart" instead of gritting my teeth and suffering.
- I'm so proud.

What's Next?

Continue to use your coping methods. Urges will arise less and less often, but when they do come, they may still be quite strong.

List the coping methods you have found most helpful and will continue to use.

_____

_____

_____

_____

_____

_____

Remember to be extra nice to yourself. To prevent post-quitting blues, or to overcome them if they occur, be extra nice to yourself—do things you want to do. Use the money you are saving by not smoking to buy luxuries that you will enjoy.

After the initial challenge of quitting, staying smoke-free can seem like a letdown. People around you may be less supportive, thinking you already have it made. So, it is up to you to pamper yourself over the next several months.

Review this guide from time to time. After being free of cigarettes for a few weeks, there is a tendency to stop doing the things that helped you quit. Keep this guidebook close by and reread selected sections to maintain your non-smoking skills. Continue to write in the guide to keep it current.

Smoking is not an option. If you goof and have a single puff on a cigarette, the chances are very high that you will return to regular smoking. No matter what crisis or temptation you face in the future, tell yourself that, "smoking is not an option." Stick by your decision to live smoke free—it is a good decision.

Quit clinics can help. For many, the support of a quit-smoking clinic is very helpful. If you are having difficulty remaining free of cigarettes, consider attending a clinic.

Many communities now have QuitSmart classes available. These classes are taught by health professionals who have been trained and certified by the author of this guide. Consult our internet home page (www.QuitSmart.com) to find a class near you. For other clinics, check your phone book's yellow pages under "Smokers' Information and Treatment Centers."

It takes experience to become skilled in helping people quit smoking, so steer away from clinics or clinic leaders who have a short history. Also, be skeptical of programs that claim long-term (six months to one year) success rates of 60 percent or more. A 50 percent success rate would be very good.

Plan an anniversary celebration. For your six-month anniversary of freedom from cigarettes, do something special. Use the hundreds of dollars that did not go up in smoke to have a party, to take a trip, or to purchase something special just for you.

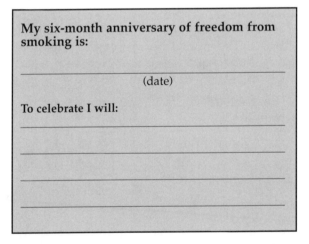

My six-month anniversary of freedom from smoking is:

_____
(date)

To celebrate I will:

_____

_____

_____

Help others. Your success may inspire others to quit. You can help them by sharing your knowledge of the quitting process, and by being supportive.

Your doctor, dentist, and company health nurse will be interested in knowing about your experience with the QuitSmart System. They want to help people quit—they see the illness and death caused by cigarettes every day. They may want to use the order form on the last page of this guide to request information about training seminars and materials to help them in counseling smokers to "QuitSmart."

You have accomplished much in reading this guide. Your success in quitting smoking may inspire you to make other healthy lifestyle changes. The routine wearing of seat belts, good eating habits, and a prudent exercise program soon become a part of many exsmokers' lives.

Be good to yourself and enjoy your new lifestyle!

Robert H. Shipley, Ph.D.

QuitSmart™ Kit

From the Director of the respected Duke University Quit Smoking Program. Over 100,000 kits are in print—a best seller in the stop-smoking market.

QuitSmart Guidebook
Reveals how to use the QuitSmart System to break the addiction/habit of smoking.

Hypnosis Audiotape
Induces relaxation and helps overcome psychological dependence on cigarettes. Available in English or Spanish.

Better Quit® Cigarette Substitute
A patented realistic cigarette substitute with adjustable draw.

Some of the Rave Reviews

> "It is hard to say which of the three kit elements I enjoyed most."
>
> Jamie Dillon, MS, RRT
> *Advance for Respiratory Care Practitioners*

> "This kit should be purchased, studied and used by all . . ."
>
> Helen Sibilano, RN, MSN
> *Oncology Nursing Forum*

> "The QuitSmart Stop Smoking Kit is easy to use, interactive and informative . . . I enthusiastically recommend the kit."
>
> Dr. Crystal Dunlevy
> *Respiratory Care*

⚲ QUIT SMART. *Order Form*

Qty.		Price
____	**QuitSmart Kit**—QuitSmart Guide, Hypnosis Tape, and Better Quit® Substitute ($25.95 each kit)	____
____	**QuitSmart Guide** ($8.99 each)	____
____	**QuitSmart Hypnosis Tape** ($12.99) (specify English or Spanish)	____
____	**Better Quit® Cigarette Substitute** ($4.99)	____
	North Carolinians add 6% sales tax.	____

Shipping: Add $5.00 for the first item or kit, plus 50¢ for each additional item.   ____

                                        Total   ____

Guarantee: You may return any item within 30 days for a full refund if not satisfied.

Method of Payment:

❑ Purchase Order # _____

❑ Check to QuitSmart   ❑ MasterCard   ❑ VISA

Acct # _____ Exp. _____

Signature _____

Name _____

Address _____

City _____

State _____ Zip _____

Daytime Phone # (____) _____
(In case we need to contact you about your order)

**Send to: QuitSmart Stop Smoking Resources, Inc.
              P.O. Box 99016, Duke Station
              Durham, NC 27708-9016**

❑ Please send information on quantity discounts.
❑ Please send information on QuitSmart Leader Certification Seminars for health professionals.

Call 1-888-73-SMART (76278) toll free